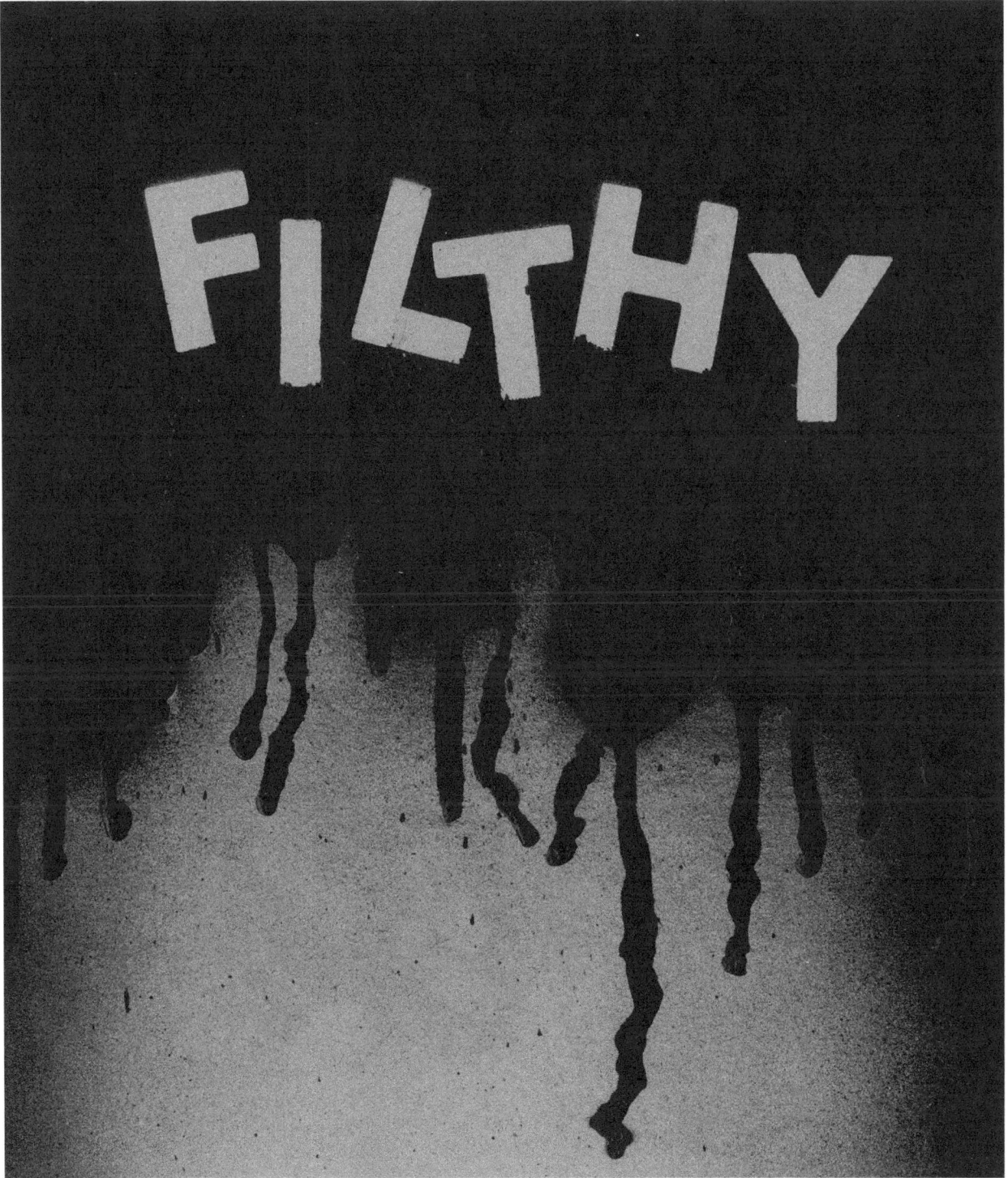

FILTHY

FILTHY

Jake Giszczynski
with art by
Dominique Jackson

ISBN: 978-1-943170-08-1

Cover Image: Dominique Jackson "Filthy"
Cover Design: Jake Giszczynski
Interior Design: Jake Giszczynski
Splatter Art: Dominique Jackson
Production Director: Jane L. Carman

Typefaces: Baskerville, Arial, Filthy Font

Published by: Lit Fest Press

Carman
688 Knox Road 900 North
Gilson, Illinois 61436
festivalwriter.org

For You.
You deserve it.

Table of Contents

A Quick Word about the Photos

Dominique Jackson has been partnering with Jake Giszczynski as an artistic team for the past six years. During this particular project, Giszczynski and Jackson worked together envisioning, staging, shooting, developing, and printing each photograph. The photos featured in this book have been shot in an eclectic array of formats, including 35mm, 120mm, and digital. Each offers a unique frame and perspective, and each comes with its own restrictions and freedoms. Every picture featured here offers up its own little story. Sometimes the stories echo a poem, and other times they complement them. Feel free to wander through the pages and explore the world they've curated for you. Just make sure you remember how to get home.

GlaxoSmithKline Kaleidoscope
[A Shitty Perspective]

uses:
builds increasing protection against painful sensitivity of teeth due to
cold heat acids sweets or contact
smoothes detangles and eliminates static
great for makeup application and blending
touching up nail polish
cleaning electronics
and delicate baby care
portable and convenient for travel
aids in the prevention of dental cavities
aids in the removal of phlegm mucus or other secretions
for washing to decrease bacteria on the skin
reduces underarm wetness
temporarily relieves itching associated with
minor skin irritations inflammation and rashes
supports heart health
useful for arts crafts and hobbies
provides relief of occasional sleeplessness
helps prevent and temporarily protects chaffed chapped or cracked skin
temporary relief of minor aches and pains of muscles and joints
helps to restore and maintain regularity
generally produces effect within 12-72 hours

First Impressions

i am not a girl
i know my hair is pretty
please don't call me "ma'am"

Keeping Up Appearances

the mingy wrinkled miser
was a great friend of the Kaiser
and his wife was none the wiser
of his sick unchristian deeds

see, when he was at home
or even on the phone
with a lady of his own
to satisfy his needs

he was gentle as a kitten
a fine lanolin mitten
his wife was surely smitten
by his playful will to please

but soon as he left the door
there were victims by the score
of behavior you'd abhor
more than an ill-directed sneeze

he'd snatch the change from bums
and lech on wide-eyed nuns
he'd block out all the sun
and tax you just to breathe

but soon as he hit the sack
his wife sure had a knack
for knocking him on his back
or better yet
his knees

David Frantz
[With Warm Regards]

born in kankakee
says his biggest regret
is living
in illinois

graduated high school in 1992
and has lived locally
here in normal
ever since

finding it difficult to juggle
full time work
academia
breathing
sleeping
eating
he took a 10-year hiatus

he is currently very career oriented

he has worked in a number
of different print shops

he is good with software

he is interested in graphic design theory
wants to be the communication line
between graphic concept
and graphic production

he is currently very career oriented

his goal is to be involved with library science
his major is in Publishing Studies
his focus is in Publishing Studies

his motto is:
"a short skirt on a windy day is proof of god's love"

he is currently very career oriented

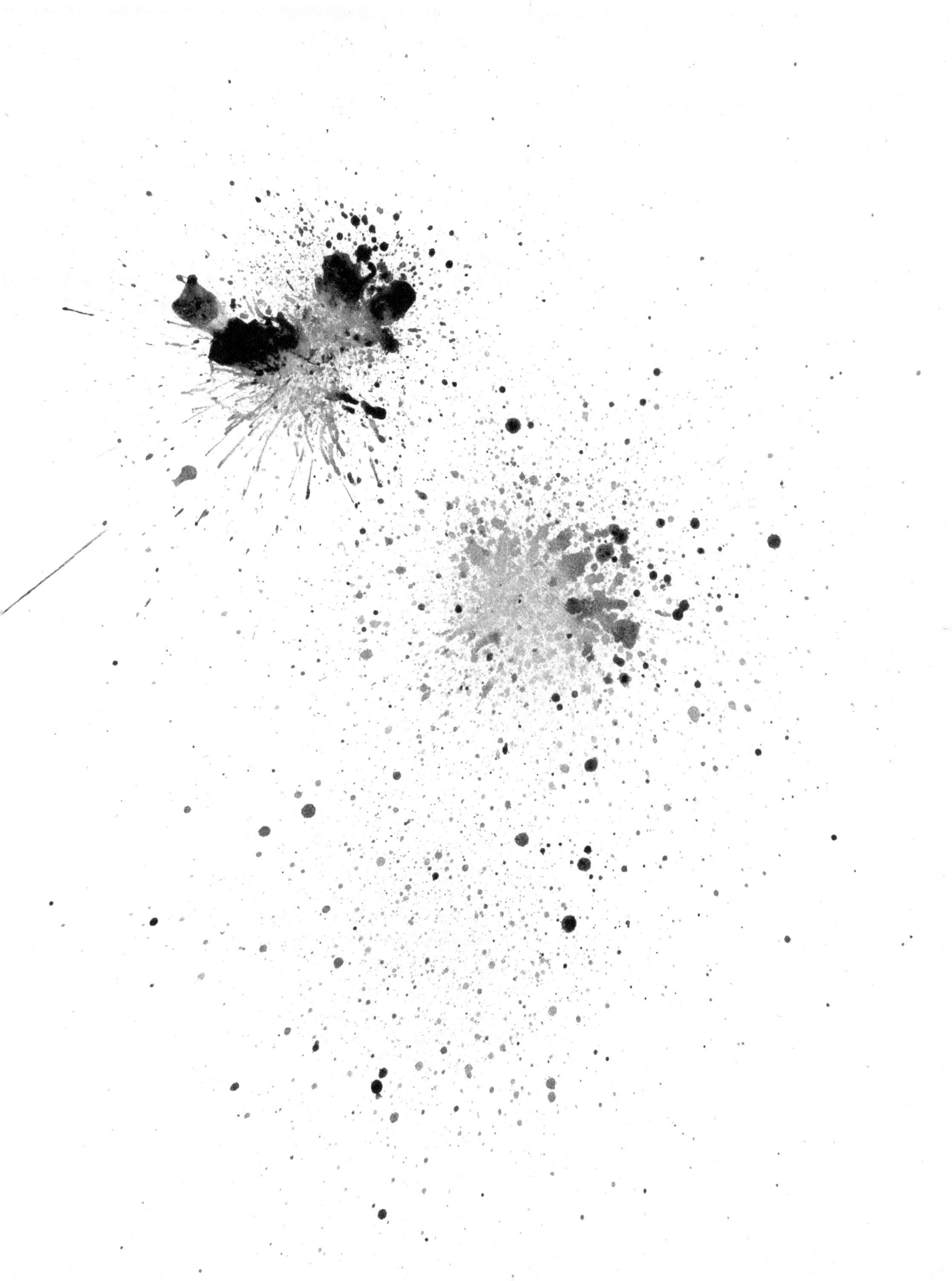

Situational Awareness

head high in the clouds
interrupted by concrete
i should look down more

Pills

ADD OCD RLS and PMS
today it just seems like everyone's a mess
but soon as you think there's nothing to do
i make a brand new pill just for you

you there the freak that yells
this new pill will save you from the bells
nevermind the side effects

[the boils the bumps the kidney failure that pain in your neck]

nevermind the fact that it could kill you
it's revolutionary
it's cheap
it's neat
it's new

if you're fat i'll stop you from eating
if you're cranky i'll spare your kids the beating
if you're lazy, i know just how to perk you up
it's all kosher if you pee in a cup

it's all legal
and if you call now the first pill's free
it's a wonderful business
bliss for you and money for me

i am the doctor with a bad taste in my mouth
the guy who buys my supplies from way down south
i take from the rich and i take from the poor
without their cash how else could i make more?

blue pills
yellow pills
new pills
and mellow pills

have an itch?
i can scratch it
can't get pregnant?
i'll help you hatch it

we're a medicated america
with 99 billion customers satisfied today
ignorance is bliss
who needs their mind anyway?

i am the peddler who deals drugs the right way
escape real life
get a scrip today

it'll only cost you an arm
a leg
a kidney
and your soul
but you'll be able to sleep now

extract your brain
i'll fill the hole

welcome to america
the first pill's free
but soon enough

your life belongs to me

Translucid

automatic zoot suit with piano key teeth and a washboard necktie tumbles
out of the alley adjusts his copper bowler hat and calls to me through a throat
filled with gravel and tar bellows

HEY BOY WANNA BUY A CAN OF BEES

and i say yes after which he proceeds to pummel me with a laptop bag filled
with soap and as i lay there bleeding and sudsy he drops a sealed tin can with
a mean humming sound and as i reach over to grasp the can i notice it is
slowly opening

Marrow Music

have you ever heard the legend
of Sue the Dinosaur
and her wanton
insatiable
blood lust?

how she's chewed children up
and spit them out
like so much zebra stripe gum
swallowed some whole
and even sat on others?

well it's true you know
the stories
they're all true
she's a towering behemoth of
rock-bones
whose only function is to

KILLKILLKILL

i was there
saw it with my own two eyes
my class went on a trip
to the chicago field museum

and campbell
i told him
no touching
the sign says no touching

but campbell
well he did what he wanted
not that he was a bad kid

just headstrong
stubborn
naïve

so he walked right up to her
doing the limbo under the guard rails
and he looked Sue right in her

massive
sunken
hollow eyes

and he poked her big toe
and us kids we all jumped
like scalded cats
cause we were sure

this time

that campbell had gone too far
that this was it
but nothing happened

no alarms went off
no security guards came running
no executive orders from the president
to lock him up and throw away the key

so we all breathed
a collective sigh of relief
but campbell
that wasn't good enough for him
he didn't want to just touch Sue
he wanted to play her
so he did
he grabbed two pencils

and he started tapping on her toes

tapatapatapatapa
tinktinktinktink

rattling around those mineral bones
like a cartoon xylophone
and he worked his way up
like some Stomp! inspired shit
and found himself
climbing up her legs
and playing her ribs

the kid was actually pretty good
he just kept pounding
and pounding
with those pencils
gathering in intensity
and ferocity

we began grabbing things
from the exhibits around us
ancient clubs
and arrowheads
and we all just started rapping
on those ancient ivories

ricky was on her snout
playing "chopsticks" on her teeth
with ming dynasty chopsticks
the irony was delicious

cambria was beating
big Sue's tail
with king tut's legs

and jon just climbed
up her back
and got to playing her spine
with the royal spoons of camelot

and i was really starting to wonder
where the fucking adults were
in all of this
when suddenly our teacher
came skittering out of the bathroom
still adjusting her skirt

security guard right behind her
still adjusting his belt

and she stretched her fingers out
as she was halfway across the room
and just as soon as her crimson lips
curled around those fateful words:

THE SIGN SAYS NO TOUCHING

a heavy rumbling poured out of Sue
and this great big ancient bitch
started SHAKING
and just like london bridge
the whole fucker came down
with all of us kids on it

one great big CRASH
and just like that
the band broke up
and campbell parks
he was on the bottom of that pile

jagged bones poking out through
a mountain of ragged bones
and a pool of blood
stretching to the walls

some of us turned out ok
and because of that
we were punished

not with survivor's guilt
or juvie hall
but four detentions
and 72 hours
of picking up old bones
and throwing out new ones
in a big gray trash bin
labeled
                    "Campbell Parks and the Troglodytes"

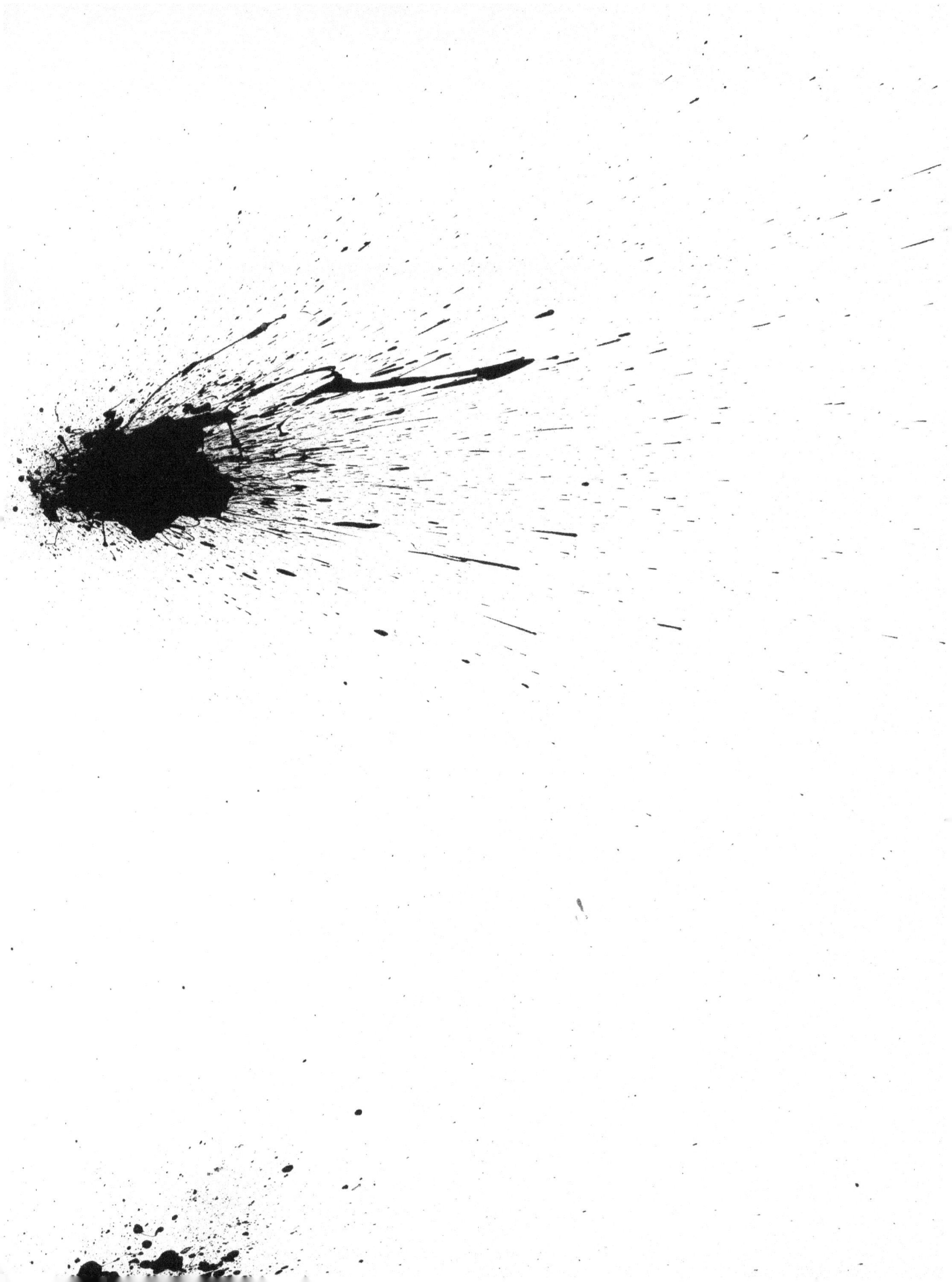

Capitalism

learning how to swim
without a single lifeguard
is a crucible

Free Market Funerals

america we have failed you
you studied
we slacked
you worked
while we snacked

you've poured your blood and sweat
into giving us the most gracious gift of all
and we've returned it for store credit

what audacity
such gall

you've sacrificed
hours
days
lives

building walls stronger than ever
impossible to dent
over them
we've painted obscenities
screaming our boredom
our ignorance
and our misguided discontent

we don't want liberty equality or fraternity
we want loudspeakers in which to bellow apathetic sighs
and demand indemnity

we want high definition surround sound wireless lazy-boys
blindly chasing the american dream
spending money we don't have to buy toys

you gave foundations
on which to build great towers
of astounding dimensions

instead we built wal-marts
strip malls
and franchises too numerous to mention

give us billions of calories
stacked to the ceiling and wrapped in petroleum
then clean up our mess
after we've spewed all over your linoleum

bring us:
cheese whiz
hot pockets
fast cars
and crotch rockets
and if we fall?
snatch our wallets
to replace the bones in our sockets

walk on us
call it an asian massage
we'll pay you gladly
then buy a new car
for the new garage

we'll buy the world!
all of us
at the same time!
we'll spend it all
'till we've spent our very last dime!

and once we're broke
let the credit cards and banks rape us for more
let the debt collectors come
knocking down our doors

we'll declare bankruptcy
just begin anew
we're all victims!
we can't help it!
we'll sue!

next thing you know
we're the ones walking on you

we'll make more money
profiting from our own ignorance
we'll sue altoids
while driving with our eyes closed
we choked on their breath mints

is this what we've been reduced to?
hamsters in wheels?
the black shadow of national ruin nips at our heels
but we don't care
we'll spend 'till we're dead
and then?

        it'll be our children's problem instead.

King George and His Gift

pre-packaged
shrink wrapped
economy sized
and vacuum packed

under sold
over priced
best served cold
and thinly sliced

tastelessly bland
but tastefully advertised
with the texture of sand
at least it comes super-sized!

hollow in the middle
but hard on the surface
sure it looks pretty
but we've forgotten its purpose

it's tough to chew
even harder to swallow
sure today it looks new
but it's rotten tomorrow

overrated
saturated
and if you're not careful
it'll leave you subjugated

hand picked
and painted pretty
then gently kicked
to every city

covered in flies
while the east burns red
it's spit in our eyes
it's capitalism
and it's dead

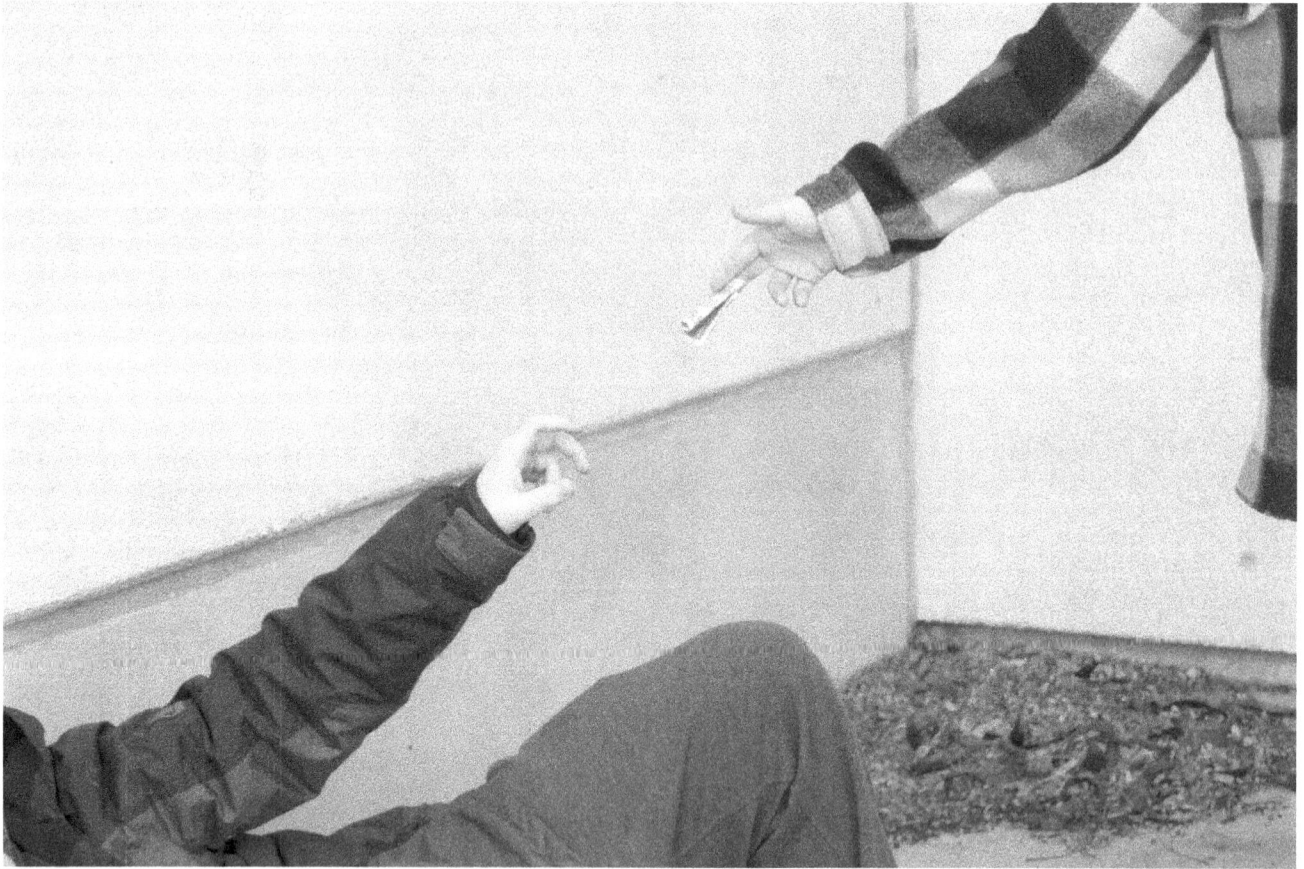

Uncle Sam

wind up tin man snake oil salesman in a hazmat suit walks with the resounding crash of DOW jones NASDAQ NYSE filibuster bailouts. inequities pour out from every step in a forest-green ooze trailing fumes of acrid blood and dirt putridity. he laughs from behind the plastic gas mask as i curdle where i stand.

Anger Management

encased in barrels
made of flimsy fiberglass
plebeians fly by

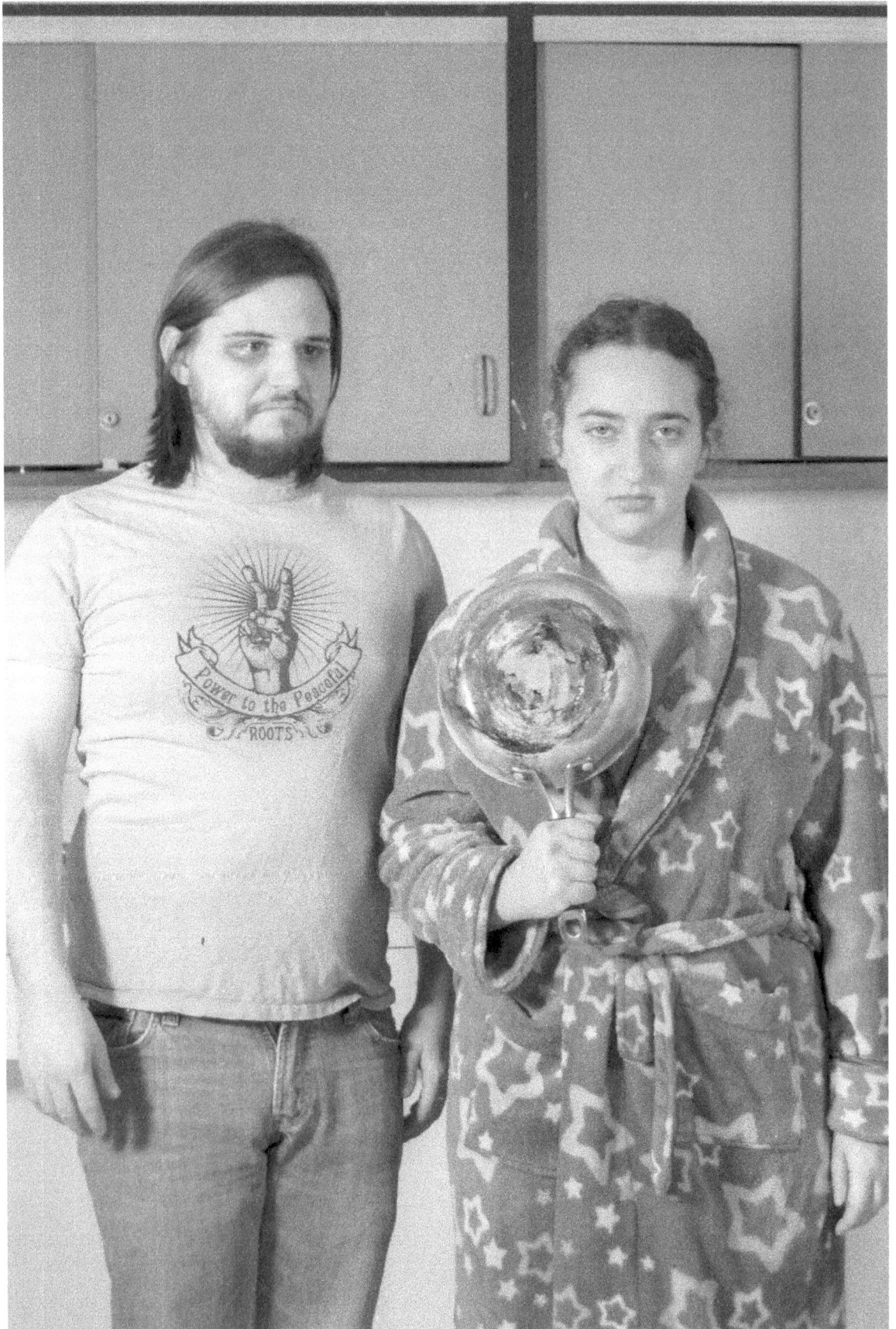

Ode to a Critic

fuck you
insolent swine
impudent strumpet

the pimples on my ass
ache for the warm sloppy embrace
of your facehole

i've been snipping paper clips
with your nail trimmer
waiting for them to bend
your nail back
hard

i burned down the shithole
you grew up in
and pissed on the ashes

then i exhumed your dog
just to throw him in a river
he's never looked better

read your yearbook
found your first girlfriend
spitroasted her
with your older brother

said she'd never squirted before then

sit on my
spit plastered
baby-batter blaster
spin for a minute or two

hop off

suck on
the afterfuck

swirl it
in your mouth

then spit it
into my asshole

                     finger the asshole

Chuckle

mob of scene kids
flailing and swinging
arms clenching fists
arc in circles overhead
while screamo blurts out of the amp
don quixote bursts in
slaughters everyone
laughs triumphantly
over his slain dragons
"Blood on the Dance Floor"

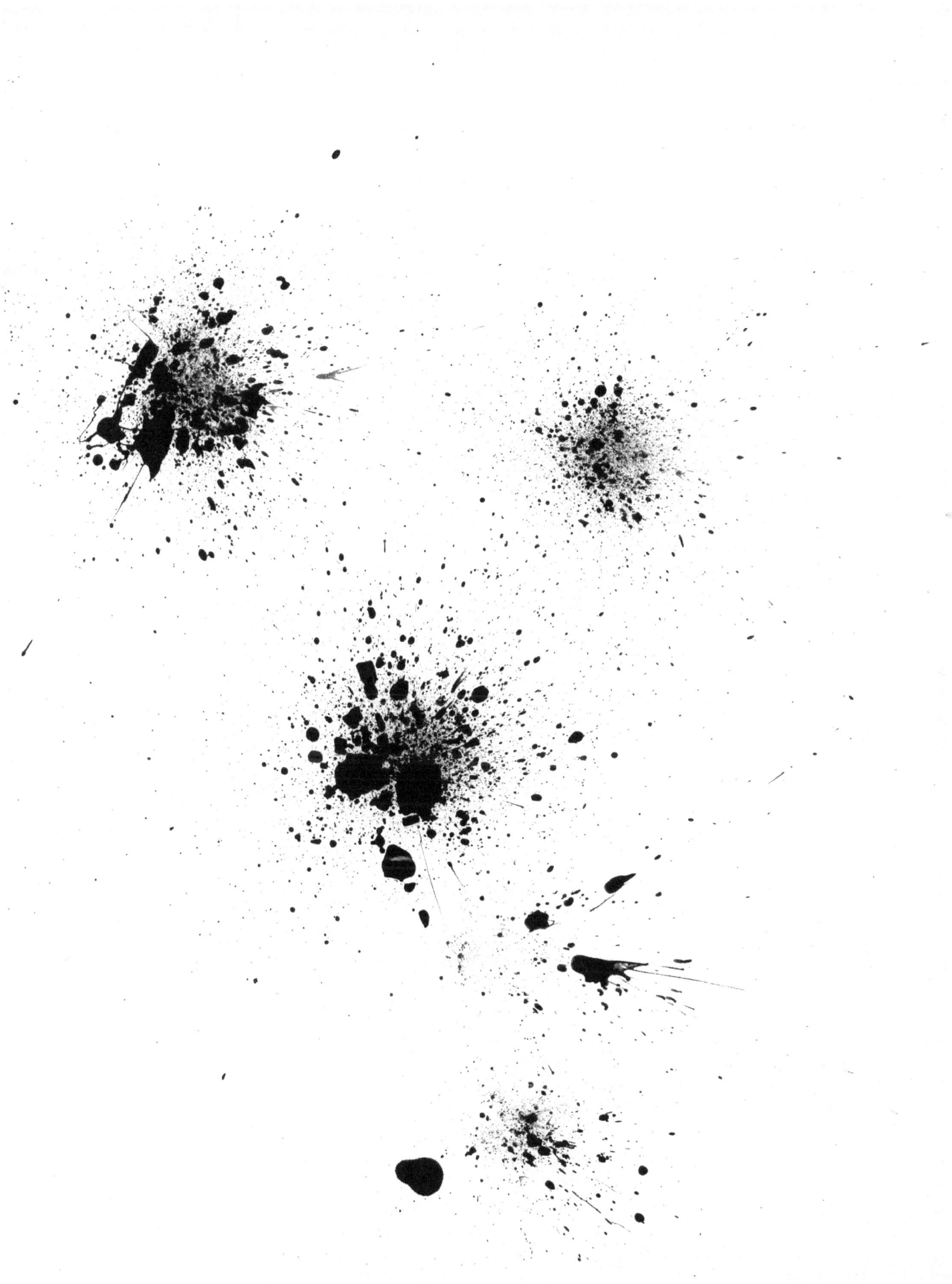

Dramatic Irony

cracking your knuckles
can be a guilty pleasure
but not for lepers

Millennial Bedlam

front door burst to cracked yellow teeth framed by cool blue smiles and the boom boom boom rattles your soul as you slide deeper deeper deeper into catatonic cacophony while pale grey smoke races across the faces of the undulating mass acid sweat smell and slippery wet skin punctuate the sin of a new generation of born again derelicts pumping designer poisons to their brains through their lungs up their nose in their veins on their tongues all the while babbling Hare Krishna Hare Krishna Krishna Krishna Hare Hare Hare Rama Hare Rama Rama Rama Hare Hare not because they know what it means but because they saw it on a coffee mug

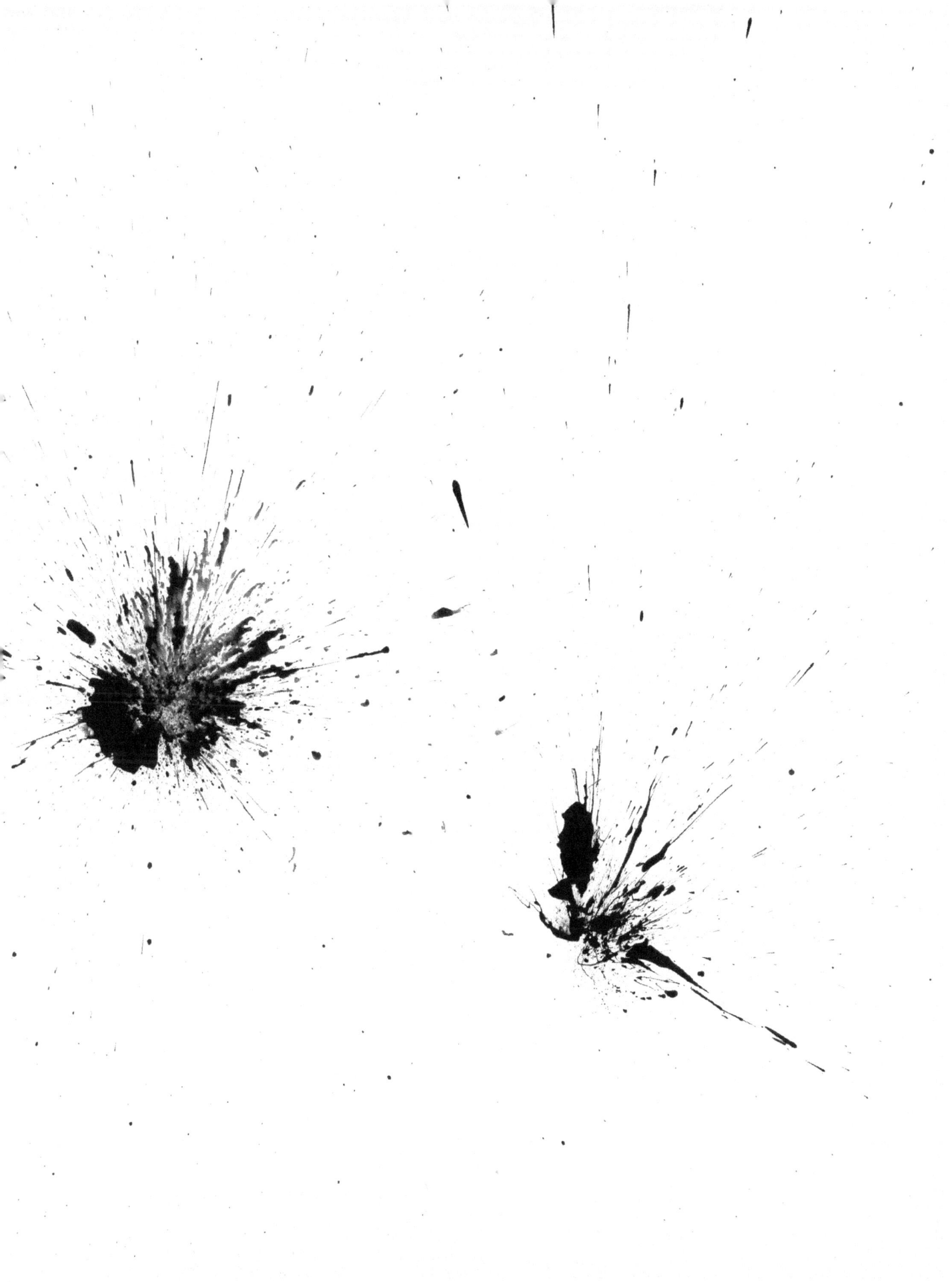

Johnson & Johnson Jamboree
[A Shitty Perspective]

directions:
fill a glass with at least 8 oz of cold water
clean the affected area
fill enclosed scoop with product
level scoop with knife or flat object
to use correctly dip a clean swab straight down into the powdery base
squeeze onto wet hands or body sponge
stroke swab gently around the outer surface
WITHOUT ENTERING THE EAR CANAL
with your pointer finger slide the inner tube all the way into the outer tube
until the ends of both tubes are even
this slides the tampon out of the applicator
and into the right place in your vagina
leave in for 1 minute
rinse thoroughly
apply at least a 1-inch thick strip of the product onto a soft bristle toothbrush
work into a lather
swish around the mouth over the affected area for at least 1 minute
and then spit out
put product in water
stir briskly
and drink promptly
apply to affected area not more than 3 to 4 times daily
children under 2 years of age:
consult a dentist or doctor

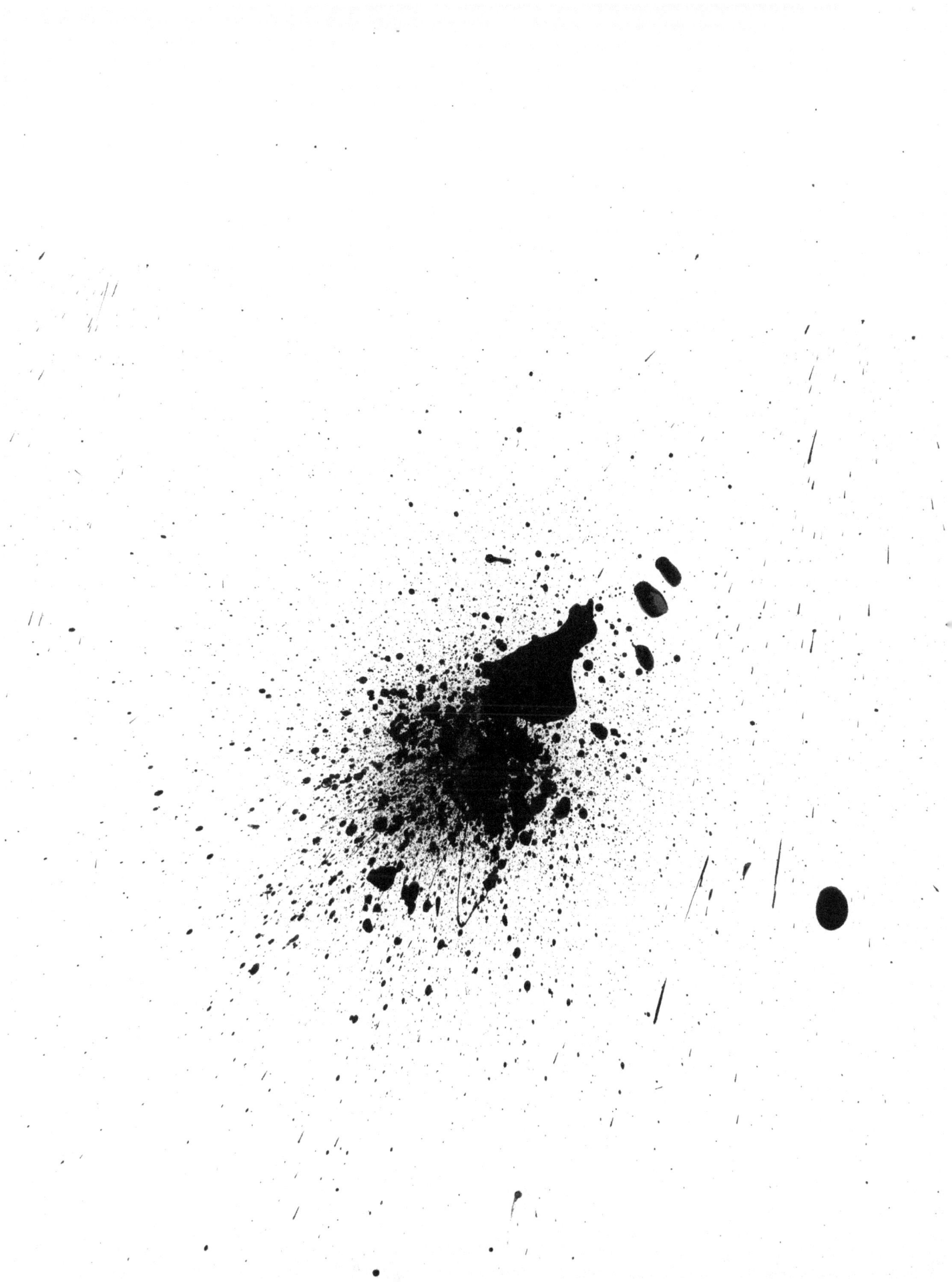

Gastrointestinal Distress

gurgle in my gut
i'm certainly not hungry
just feeling soupy

Coffee and Bagel News, Blues, and All That Jazz

Remember GURT: Greet, Upsell, Repeat, Thank
SMILE!
large coffee $2.25
plain bagel plain cream cheese
caramel macchiato skim no whip
We Gladly Learn and Teach
bacon egg and cheddar bagel
breakfast all day
SMILE!
large pumpkin latte whole add espresso add whip
Educating Illinois
Priorities for Illinois' first public university
iced chai soy add whip
club mex wrap extra onion
Passion with Purpose
SMILE!
We Gladly Learn and Teach

Source text found at:
ilstu.edu
Einstein Brothers Bagels menu and call board
WGLT 89.1 FM
Milner Library stained glass ISU emblem

iPood
iAm consumer
iAm veracity
iAm gurgling
iAm hole
iAm the chew
the bite
the tear
iAm the grind
and the mash
iAm swallow
iAm process
iProcess
iTake
iAm take apart
iAm reassemble
iAm reinvent
iDecompress
iAm compress
iAm reroute
iAm partition
iAm unzip
iAm bad gateway
iZip
iAm
down
load

Cryogenic Dinner Blues

the ice cream truck blares house music as electric children dance behind wav-
ing colors amongst sweating stinking revelry and their parents all rush home
to catch their favorite strip the only strip you'll ever need it's real it's live they
just turn on the cameras and you melt in ecstasy
curfew call and the music stops as the children come home to catch cugger-
mugger about "where've they been" and "what a shame" the tubes flicker off
as the sun sets everyone settles in and everything starts to freeze again 500
more years waiting for the next episode the next delicious scoop but don't you
worry because
they won't feel a thing.

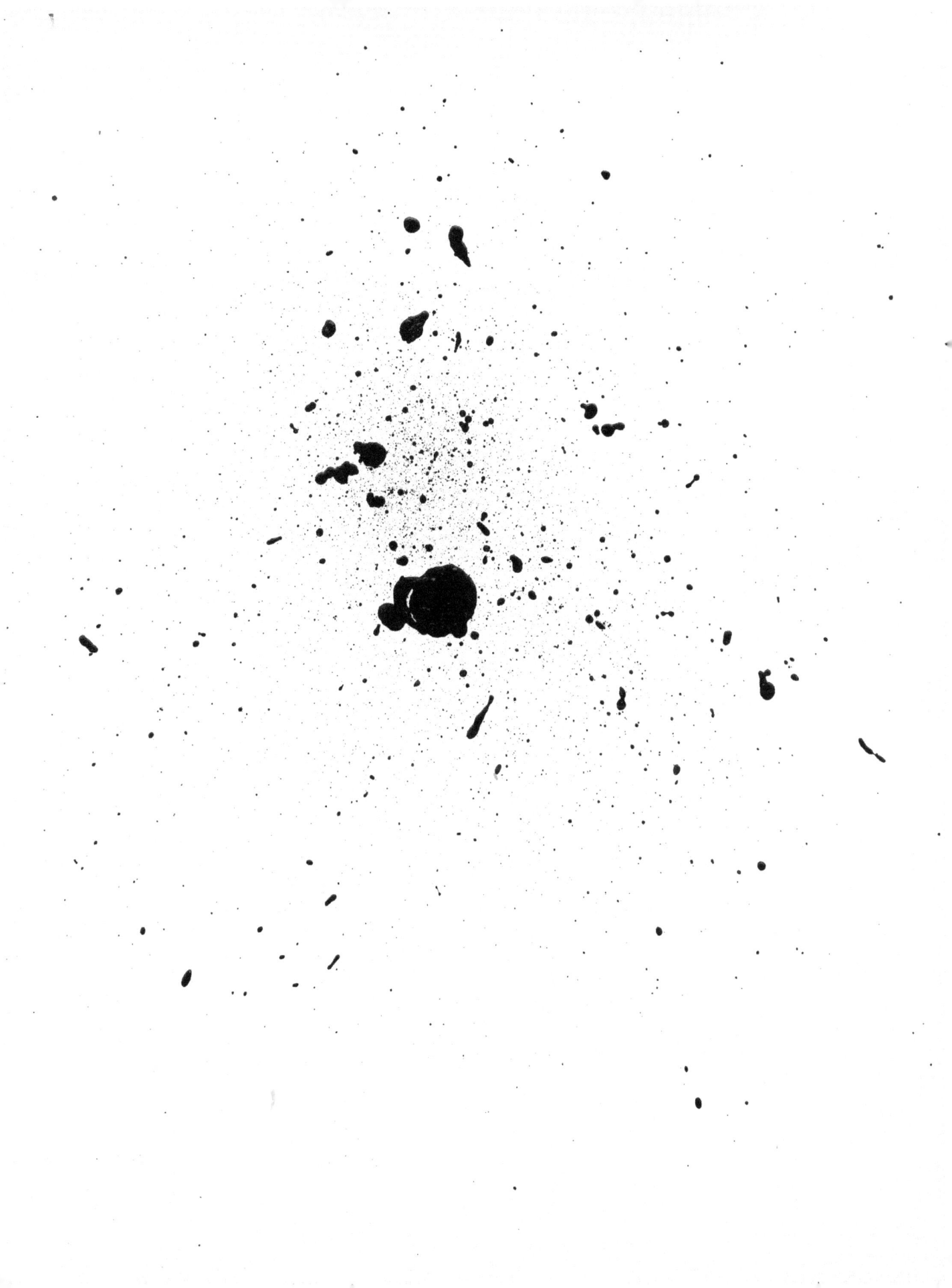

Patience

cup touches my lips
searing pain jumps to my face
burned my tongue again

The Great White North

my father grew up in hamtramck michigan
just outside of the city
"pole-town" they called it
because of all us Polacks

being so close to the border
my family became accustomed to
frequent trips North
to windsor canada

that carried on into my early childhood
with the trips going farther
and farther
every time

windsor, so my grandpa could gamble
and quebec, so dad could explore
and grandma could buy all the
little tchotchkes in the shops

the whole time i was there
i kept hearing all this fuss
about how the first nation
are treated better than our
native americans

how the first nation have been preserved
and given all due respect
and everything is fine now
and they are getting better every day

but the tchotchkes on the shelves
were little inuit eskimos
with big puffy parkas

slanted squinted eyes
and spears with fish

and the reservations
or communities
or whatever they call them there
we all passed on the way?

i saw the same sadness i saw
on different road trips
to our beautiful
american Southwest

i saw empty liquor bottles on the road
families pushing carts
plummeting speed limits
[revenue has to come from somewhere]

sure i saw smiles too
inuits wearing blue jeans
t shirts and shoes without
tennis rackets on the bottom

but it seemed to me
even then, at my young age
that "first nation"
was just another word for "indian"

that cigar store effigies
had been replaced
with stone and marble statuettes
much smaller
                but far more marketable to tourists.

Punch Drunk Preacher

the paper mâché man screams gospel rings out in symphony while the heavens drip sapphire and the sun bleeds matchstick fire Sister Susan and young McKenzie family gather to absorb sermon and glorious weather the smell of mud grass and sunshine permeates their skin but the words just bounce right off

Epiphany

it's chilly one night in the somber month of october
and creatures grow restless in their concrete cages
sign on the door says:
only 21 and over
but hyenas know bouncer won't check their ages

inside gorilla beats his chest
when it comes to billiards
he knows who's best

at the bar
vultures search for another drunken doe
herd seems a little thin tonight though

in glides rippling lion
females flock from left and right
while lonely timid elephant
sobs at the magnificent sight

rooster crows
chest filled with pride
unaware his hen is off
with that other cock clyde

jackass argues blindly with owl
hasn't lost yet
dodo watches game intently
placing another bet

wolf howls at vixen's half moon
calling it to attention of pack around room

half-jungle gathered
around the watering hole

little do they realize
the Zookeeper is in control

at 5 dollars per saucer
how can the alley cat afford his cream?
yet he drinks till his belly
bursts at the seams

birds squawk and lions roar
that hen sleeping with your friend is still a whore
stagger out of the pub with a dazed look of fright
disappointed to learn

we're all animals at night

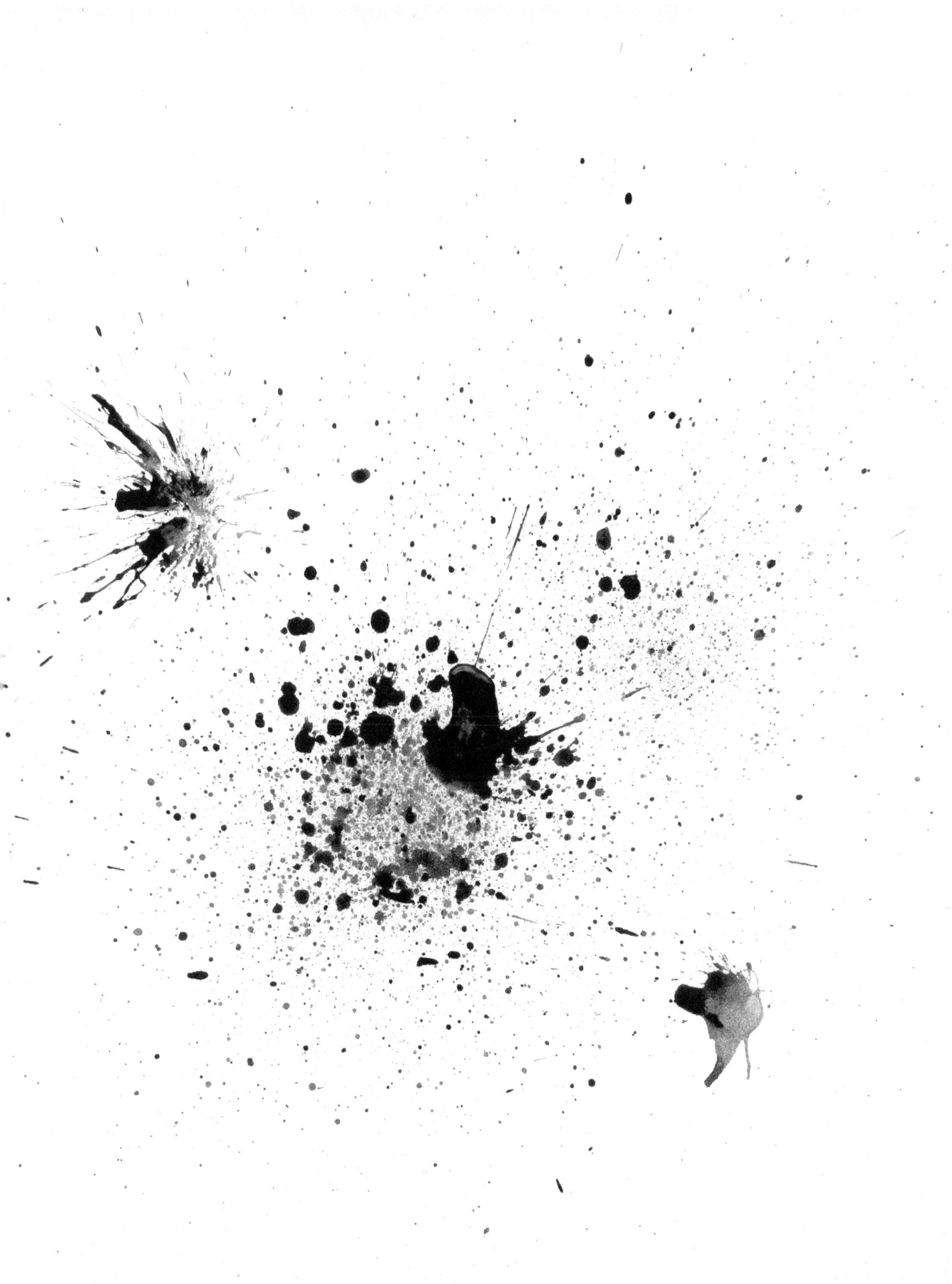

Inheritance

my mom is crazy
just look at the evidence
[i get it from her]

Inflate This

everything is harrying
officials are tarrying
and citizens are carrying
the brunt of all the weight

but who will know the score
after twitter guerrillas bore
to the heart of every sore
that festers and pulsates

the pustules will pop
as the house and senate rock
and the people suck the cocks
of the politician state

Historical Fanfiction

jefferson turns down offer
for extra muscle
from colonial mercenaries
signs declaration instead
thinking
"we're all reasonable people here"

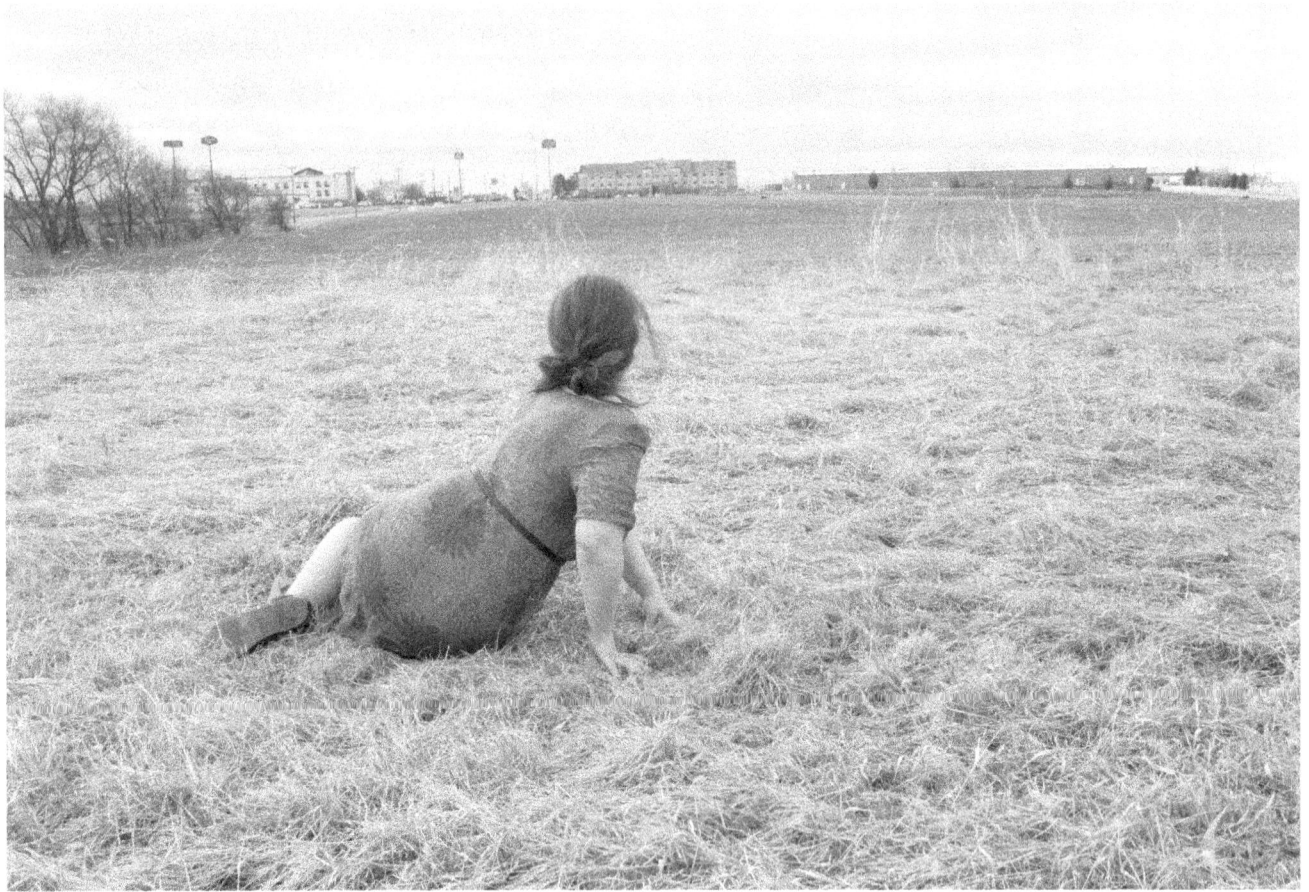

Technicolor Lackluster

blue and red collide
scattering reason far and wide
colors clash and scream their pride
even amongst friends
ignorance cannot hide

reason fades
with cities razed
culture is made
moments later
in its deathbed it's laid

covered in war paint
the savages came
each of them unaware
that they're all the same

without unity the tribe will fall

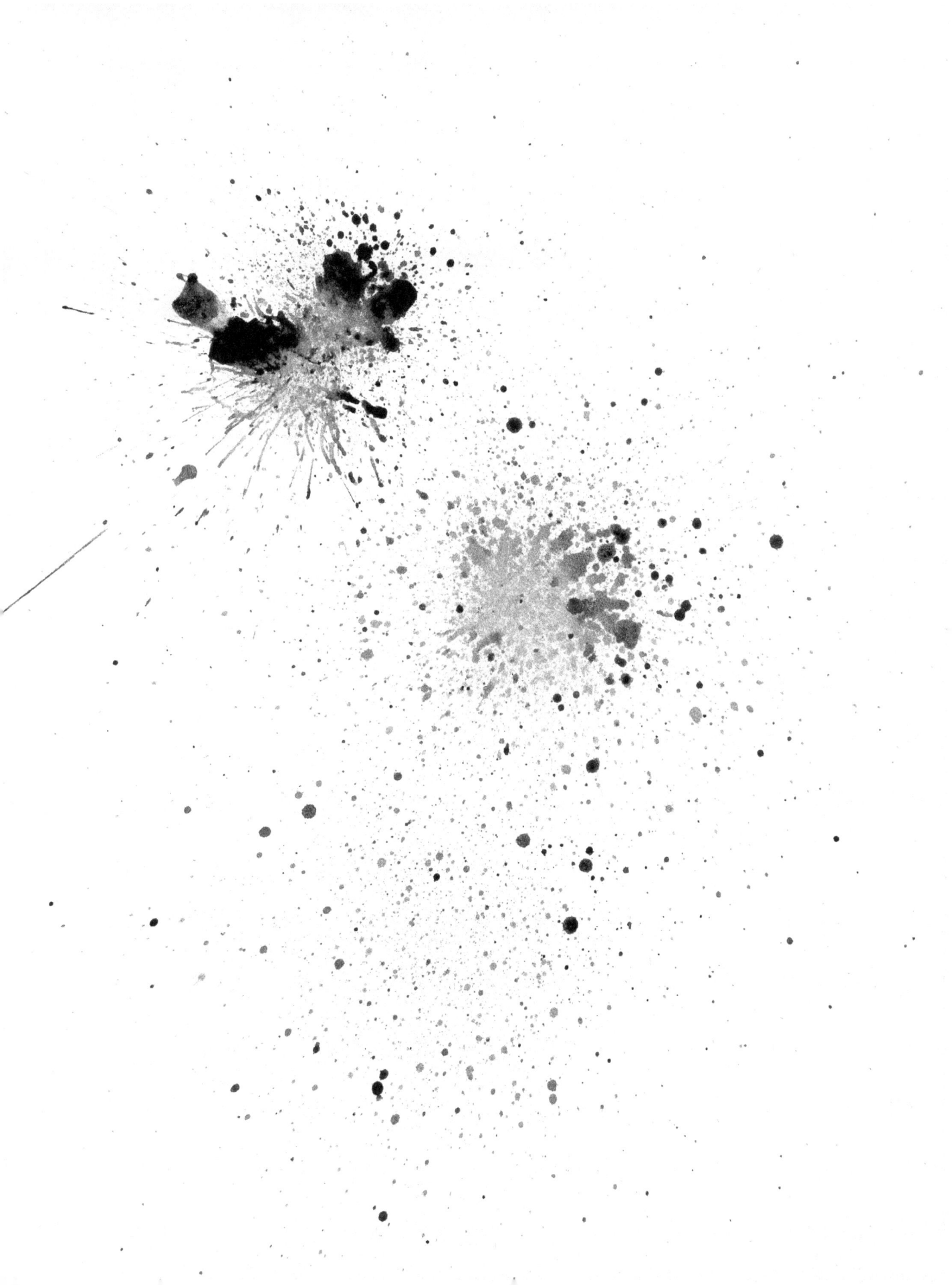

Kafka

woke up on christmas
dad sculpted me an ashtray
he is such a child

Carnal Grotesque

your legs tremble with anticipation as the
gimp suit man lurches toward you
grabs your waist
and dances elegantly

his cold black fingers
crack and creak in yours
as he clutches you oh-so-closely
you whisper "Take me Frankenstein"

as the zippered mouth bursts
and his mangled leather face plunges into your neck
blood starts to trickle
as aluminum teeth rend and tear
your vision fades to black

awaken sharply
cold and sticky
as your maroon scabs weep
and your head aches
with his resounding laughter

he stole your innocence
with reckless abandon

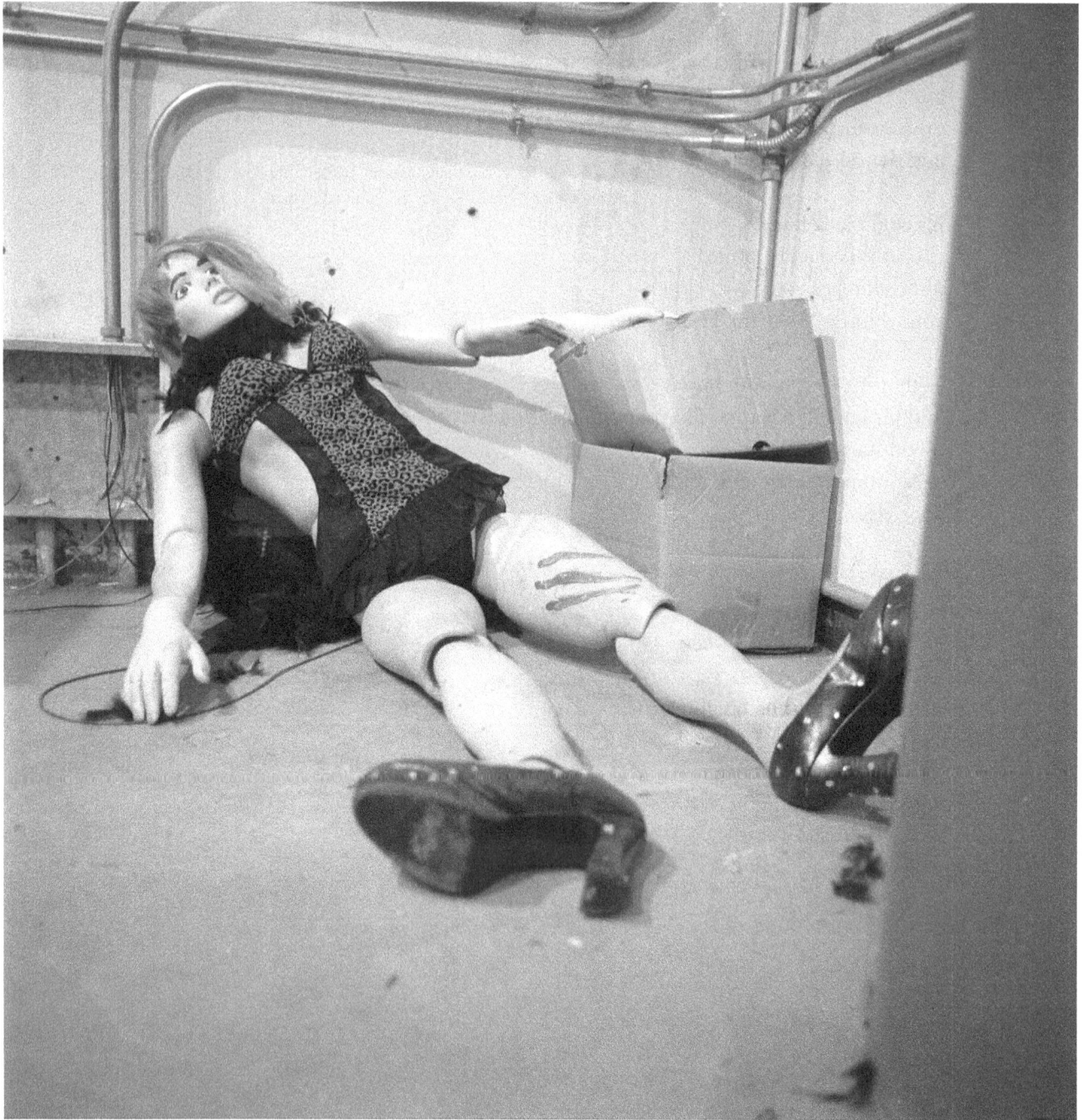

Tribute

worship me
        lift me up high
             weep
                     at my baroque thighs
                         tear the sweet meat from my carcass
                         salt it
                         rub it
                                 hang it in the sun
                         eat me
                         shit me
                    save the shit
               my bones
           cover them in plaster
        erect me
in repose
        mold me
            chisel me
               drill me
               but don't fill me
                    leave the hole
                       so the wind can
                           whistle through me

                           statuary gape

Ted

it's late. i'm late. cold dew clinging to the boot. loose howls flung caroming off bars and houses. frosty glaze on grass on parked cars on rusty leaves. a crunch to the step. spent cigarette scuttles like a wild loose ellipses. realize too late that i cannot mix vodka and redbull with only a swish of the can. half cringing trying to gulp down as i push open double doors to centennial. a hurried pace. sticky brow glues hair haphazard. red cheeks large spots under arms. faint smell of onions of microwaved mustard of mild nondescript cheese. sole echo throughout sheer vacancy.

stairs. steady clomp to top floor. warm yellow billowing into hall. just like my first time. listless waves obligatory smiles. an ass out hug. scratch of disused pen on stubble table. one hour and forty three minutes sitting and listening with droopy red eyes.
crackle of card stock. saliva on thumb.
a pregnant pause. a poem.
it's 2am and i think i might vomit.
they clap. i smile.

i go home.

Smile

i love my girlfriend
were she a hat, she'd be worn
despite miss manners

A Funny Moment of Strange Intimacy

two naked people
running around a bathroom
giggling
and whipping each other
with towels

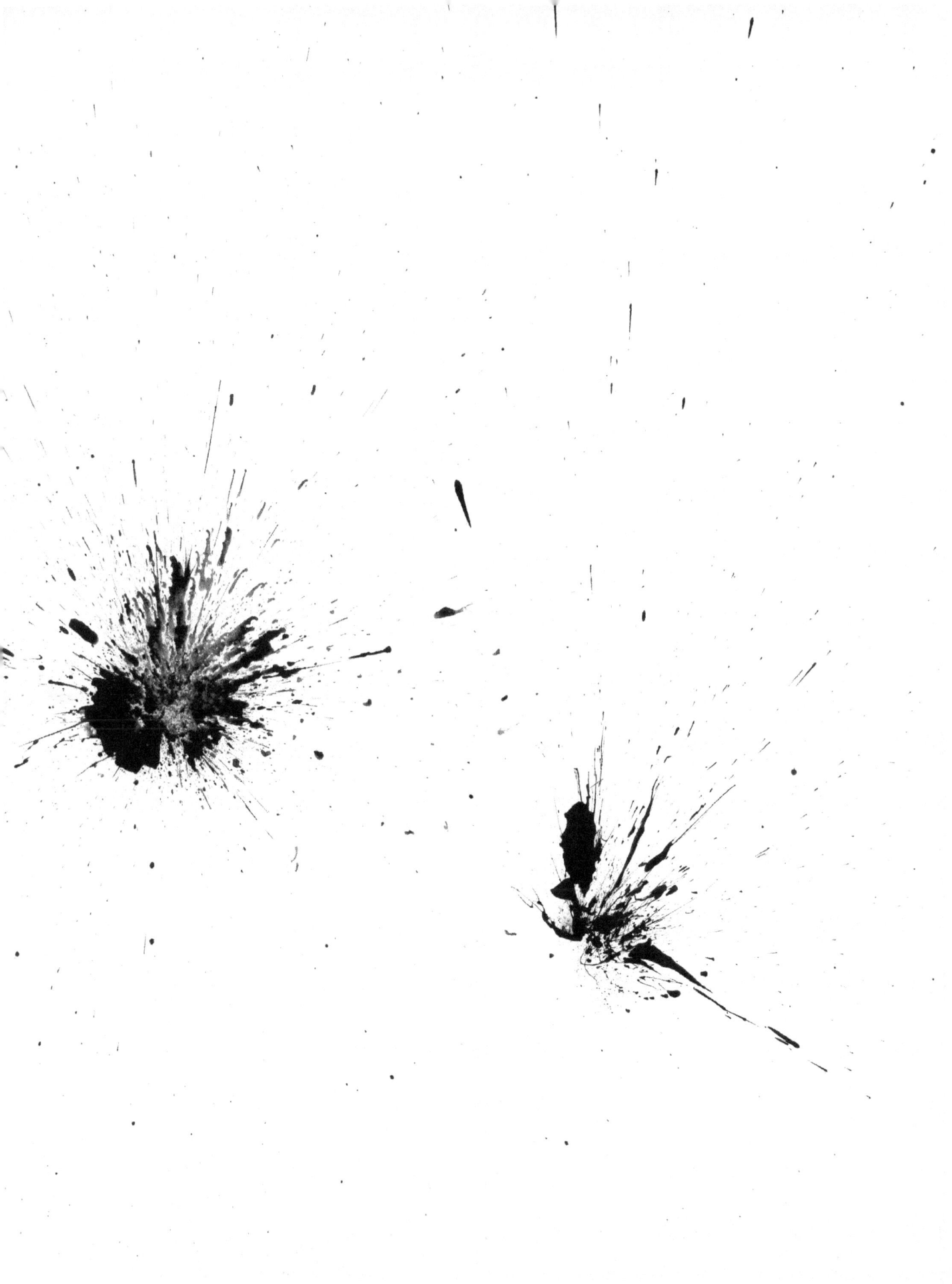

Proctor & Gamble Postmortem
[A Shitty Perspective]

warnings:
do not use
in the eyes
or apply over large areas of the body
if more than used for brushing is accidentally swallowed
get medical help or contact a poison control center
right away
do not use on broken skin
do not take at the same time
as aluminum or magnesium antacids
do not use more than directed unless told to do so by a doctor
do not use in the genital area if you have a vaginal discharge
consult a doctor
do not use if you have trouble or pain swallowing food
vomiting with blood
or bloody or black stools
these may be signs of a serious condition
see your doctor
keep powder away from the child's face
to avoid inhalation
which can cause breathing problems
taking this product without adequate fluid
may cause it to swell
and block your throat or esophagus
and may cause choking
do not put directly into the rectum
by using fingers or any mechanical device
or applicator
if you experience chest pain
vomiting
or difficulty swallowing or breathing
after taking this product
seek immediate medical attention

stop use and ask a doctor if
you get nervous dizzy or sleepless
rectal bleeding occurs
if irritation or rash occurs
if problem persists for more than 7 days
KEEP OUT OF REACH OF CHILDREN

'

Dominique Jackson is a classically trained photographer hailing from the Chicagoland area. Well-versed in analog and digital formats, she enjoys both the hands-on experience of shooting, developing, and printing her own film as well as the limitless freedom afforded by modern technology. Years of experience with acting and directing have given her a unique ability to tell a story using only a single image. She has been featured at Illinois State's University Galleries and currently shoots events in the McLean County area.

Jake Giszczynski is an emerging poet with a specialization in all that is divinely disgusting. From the ethereal ephemera of a stranger's sour breath to the visceral abjection felt for a far-flung piece of chewed wet mouthfood, he's a firm believer in capturing the moments that make our skin crawl, our groins sweat profusely, and our hair stand on end. If you experience headaches, dizziness, fatigue, dry mouth, shortness of breath, or hot bowel movements, seek immediate medical attention. Don't forget to wash behind your ears.

www.ingramcontent.com/pod-product-compliance
Lightning Source LLC
Chambersburg PA
CBHW081139090426
42736CB00018B/3408